The Bike

A story about a bike that really mattered

This is the story of an eight-year-old boy who finds himself living at home during World War II. The important question he has is "What can an eight-year-old possibly do to have the bike power to get to the 7:00 AM mass each day if he is chosen to be an altar boy?

Problem solvers across the world would tell the eight-year-old young man *to get yourself a bike son as it solves all problems for young people.* But, HOW? That was the big dilemma when most metal was diverted for the victory effort. Everybody sacrificed for America.

This story is true. But we won't tell you how it ends so you can enjoy it as John P. Lammers wrote it. All things in life do not happen as they are supposed to happen.

Nothing in life that is worth having is easy. You will enjoy reading about how this young man, never asking for more than life could provide finds a miracle solution to an almost insurmountable problem.

You won't want to put this book down. It will give you a smile that you will keep all year long.

JOHN P. LAMMERS

Copyright © Dec 2017, John P. Lammers
Title: The Bike
Subtitle: A **story about a bike that really mattered**

Publisher: Brian P. Kelly
Author: John P. Lammers

All rights reserved: No part of this book may be reproduced or transmitted in any form, or by any means, electronic or mechanical, including photocopying, recording, scanning, faxing, or by any information storage and retrieval system, without permission from the publisher, LETS GO PUBLISH, in writing.

Disclaimer: Though judicious care was taken throughout the writing and the publication of this work that the information contained herein is accurate, there is no expressed or implied warranty that all information in this book is 100% correct. Therefore, neither LETS GO PUBLISH, nor the author accepts liability for any use of this work.

Trademarks: A number of products and names referenced in this book are trade names and trademarks of their respective companies.

Referenced Material: *Standard Disclaimer:* The information in this book has been obtained through personal and third party observations, interviews, and copious research. Where unique information has been provided or extracted from other sources, those sources are acknowledged within the text of the book itself or at the end of the chapter in the Sources Section. Thus, there are no formal footnotes nor is there a bibliography section. Any picture that does not have a source was taken from various sites on the Internet with no credit attached. If resource owners would like credit in the next printing, please email publisher.

Published by:
Publisher
Email:
Web site

LETS GO PUBLISH!
Brian P. Kelly
info@letsgopublish.com
www.letsgopublish.com

Library of Congress Copyright Information Pending
Book Cover Design by Brian W. Kelly
Editor—Brian P. Kelly

ISBN Information: The International Standard Book Number (ISBN) is a unique machine-readable identification number, which marks any book unmistakably. The ISBN is the clear standard in the book industry. 159 countries and territories are officially ISBN members. The Official ISBN For this book is on the outside cover:
ISBN 978-1-947402-22-5

The price for this work is: USD	$7.95

10   9   8   7   6   5   4   3   2   1

Release Date: December 2017

Publisher's Note: *Please check out www.letsgopublish.com for BK books & to read the latest version of my heartfelt acknowledgments updated for this book. Click the bottom item of the Main menu!*

Merry Christmas

My name is:

_____

iv   The Bike

Dedication

Special thanks are extended:

To the Lammers Family for being so special

Table of Contents

Chapter 1 A Tough Life Without a Bike............... 9

Chapter 2 No Way Could I Get a Bike 15

Chapter 3 Must Be One Heck of a Friend......... 19

Chapter 4 I Always Believed in Miracles 23

Chapter 5 Bike Owner Required Skills 27

Chapter 6 A Memorable Event for Boy & Bike 33

Chapter 7 What Did That Bike Really Know?. 37

Other books by Let's Go Publish! 40

Chapter 1 A Tough Life Without a Bike

It was tough everywhere

It was the beginning of summer and I was eight years old and going into the fourth grade at St. Francis School in Ridgefield Park, NJ. The year 1943 was not a good one in America. The War was raging on two continents and here in the US, where we were free of conflict, we were asked to make a number of sacrifices on behalf of the war effort.

Sugar, butter and meat were rationed and the ration stamps that were issued by the government were required before those items could be gotten from the local Safeway or Palmer Bros. Market, both on Queen Anne Road and only a short walk through the "lots".

The "lots" were a sandlot where we played our baseball and where Mr. DeAngelo, the local shoemaker, had his victory garden in deep left field.

If you cut across center and right field along the churchyard fence that separated the property of the Reformed Church on Arthur St. from our ball field you came out on Queen Anne Road.

I must have made that trip thousands of times. "Jackie, go to the Safeway and get two quarts of milk and a loaf of bread". "And stop at Mrs. Specht's Bakery and get three French rolls for your father's lunch".

All the traveling I did was on foot because I didn't have a two-wheeler. So, it was shanks mare that took me wherever I had to go.

The half-mile walk to St. Francis four times a day—we always went home for lunch—and all those trips to the store kept my skinny frame from ever gaining an ounce.

Then there was the prospect of becoming an altar boy, which meant I would be making the trip down Bergen Ave. even more often.

You had to be in the fourth grade before Father Butscher would let you be an altar boy. My time had come. I wanted a bike in the worst way. How else was I going to be able to serve the seven o'clock Mass, get home for breakfast and then back to school on time?

Chapter 2 No Way Could I Get a Bike

Shortages, Shortages, Shortages

There were few bikes to be had because, in addition to the shortage of foodstuffs, the metal was going to make planes, ships and weapons to be used on my distant relatives in Germany. I wondered if the German boys had bikes.

There seemed to be no chance that I would ever jump on the pedal and swing my leg over the back of a bike and onto the seat that would take me wherever I wanted to go.

Then, one Saturday, when I returned from our usual game in the "lots", I couldn't help but notice some strange activity in the garage. Dad was in there working on what looked like to me the frame of a two-wheeler.

There was no doubt about it. There was a gray device, made of steel tubes, that was definitely the beginning of a bike. The only trouble was there was only a sprocket to go with it and, without other vital parts, it could never become a bike, and there were no other parts to be seen anywhere.

"Dad, what are you doing"? He said, "I got this frame in Sears and I am trying to see if I can make it into a bike".

"Where are the handle bars and wheels and all the other parts?" "I don't have them yet but I am looking around for some that will work".

"Who is it going to be for when it is finished?"

"A friend." My heart sank. Here I am, of two-wheeler age and still walking all over Ridgefield Park and my father is making a bike for a friend. I would never be free.

Chapter 3 Must Be One Heck of a Friend

Why is Dad working so hard?

As the summer went on more parts showed up in the garage and Dad worked them into what was looking more and more like prime transportation for an eight year old. And each time I asked the question the answer was the same. "I am making it for a friend".

The time came in July when we made our annual trip to Massachusetts to visit my grandmother and we left the bike in the garage almost complete except for the wheels. It now had a sprocket, a fork, handle bars and fenders.

I still had hope that I would have a bike but what good was it without wheels? I underestimated my father. Somehow, in

Webster, Mass., he had managed to find two 26" wheels, the perfect size for the bike in the garage, get them home and install them without my knowing and on the following Saturday, there it was, complete and ready to go.

Now what?

Chapter 4 I Always Believed in Miracles

Should I try out the friend's bike?

He asked me if I wanted to try it out. Now, I had never ridden a two-wheeler before so I couldn't try it unless he helped. He put me on the seat and guided me out of the driveway and onto Tessen St. He held me steady while I pedaled for all I was worth, swerving back and forth and occasionally bouncing off the curb.

The Bike

JOHN P. LAMMERS
TEANECK, NJ - C 1947

By the time we made two trips down to Park Ave. and back I had it cold and was propelling myself with great delight and much pride. "How do you like it", he said.

"It's a great bike, I wish I had one like it". "Do you want it?" "Yes". "Then it's yours". "I thought you made it for a friend". "I did".

Chapter 5 Becoming a Bike Owner Required Skills

Who would take care of the Bike?

Me?

Of course, maintenance of the bike was my job and, after a few lessons from Dad, I could take care of it myself. I could fix flats, adjust the chain, the handlebars and the fork and even take apart and repair the Bendix coaster brake, which had about a thousand parts.

Editor's Note: *As a kid, I too could work inside the intricacies of the back wheel, which was responsible for stopping when triggered. However, in my neighborhood, the bike guys would only work on New Departure Brakes sets as they were very easy to correct issues, but they broke a lot. The Bendix back wheel sprocket was huge compared to New Departure because the Bendix people probably figure out how to make a foot-brake system that would not be in constant repair.*

Anybody who could work on one of those contrivances has my eternal respect.

Although, the first couple of times I tried to fix it Dad had to come to the rescue. With endless patience he showed me how to put it back together until I could do it myself.

Editor: *I am impressed.*

I still don't know where Dad got all the parts but I suspect he scrounged some of them from his friends and from people on his mail route. His son was not going to be without a bike regardless of the difficult times and the seemingly insurmountable problem of getting one during the war. But, for a man who loved his son, the problems were there to be overcome and overcome them he did with great persistence and much love in his heart.

Now I was ready to travel and did I cover ground. The schoolyard at St. Francis had an entrance on Bergen Ave. and it was down that street that I roared and, turning through the opening in the fence, jammed on the breaks to see how long a skid mark I could leave in the cinders.

This was the standard entry for those of us who had bikes. The Nuns loved that, of course, but we took the heat in order to win the skid contest and show off a bit.

The bike, in addition to carrying me to and from school and the stores, took me all over southern Bergen County. In those days it was safe for children to travel freely and we took full advantage of the freedom.

We went to Englewood to play ball against the boys at St. Cecelia's and to Central Park in Teaneck to play the St. Anastasia team. Many of the boys I played against then later became my teammates on the St. Cecilia H.S. teams.

Chapter 6 A Memorable Event for a Boy and a Bike

The war is over

One of the most memorable bike events took place on 14 August 1945. I was on the bike on Bergen Ave. heading to St. Francis Rectory to see Father Butscher.

Ridgefield Park had a volunteer fire department and whenever there was a fire the sirens on every firehouse in town would blare the alarm, which was always the number of the box on which the alarm was turned in.

As I approached Hazelton St. they started and the sudden blast of sound from every corner of town almost knocked me off the bike. Usually the number sequence would be sounded three of four times but this time there was no box number and the blasts continued and were still going when I got to the rectory on Mt. Vernon St.

As I pulled up to a screeching halt in front of the rectory Father was on the front porch in a very excited state.

"Father, why are the fire alarms going off?"

"Jack, the war is over, it has just been announced on the radio."

Whatever I was to see Father about was soon forgotten in the jubilation that erupted on every street in town. Four years of senseless slaughter, an idea that I was too young to grasp, was ended and the men would be coming back to The Park.

14 August is my mother's birthday but also of interest is the fact that, in the Pacific, the date was already the 15th, which is the feast of the Assumption of Our Lady and the war began when the date in Japan was 8 December, the feast of The Immaculate Conception.

Do you think She was telling us that we should have paid more attention to Her message at Fatima?

Chapter 7 What Did That Bike Really Know?

Will the bike ever tell?

That bike, made by a man who loved his son, gave me more joy than I had any right to have.

The fact that he made it just for me didn't really sink in until I was a little older and mature enough to realize how easy it would have been for him to take the easy way and just tell me that, because of the war, getting a bike was impossible.

For my father doing that would have been impossible.

Thank you Mom and Dad for a great life!

John P. Lammers

Merry Christmas

Chapter 7 What Did That Bike Really Know?

Other books by Let's Go Publish!: (amazon.com, and Kindle)

Please take a run out to amazon.com/author/brianwkelly when you have time to find another book that you might enjoy.

Midnight Mass by John P. Lammers Great Christmas experiences of a young altar boy.
The Bill of Rights By Founder James Madison Refresh *your knowledge of specific rights granted to all*
Great Players in Army Football Great Army Football played by great players..
Great Coaches in Army Football Army's coaches are all great.
Great Moments in Army Football Army Football at its best.
Great Moments in Florida Gators Football Gators Football from the start. This is the book.
Great Moments in Clemson Football CU Football at its best. This is the book.
Great Moments in Florida Gators Football Gators Football from the start. This is the book.
The Constitution Companion. A Guide to Reading and Comprehending the Constitution
The Constitution by Hamilton, Jefferson, & Madison – Big type and in English
PATERNO: The Dark Days After Win # 409. Sky began to fall within days of win # 409.
JoePa 409 Victories: Say No More! Winningest Division I-A football coach ever
American College Football: The Beginning From before day one football was played.
Great Coaches in Alabama Football Challenging the coaches of every other program!
Great Coaches in Penn State Football the Best Coaches in PSU's football program
Great Players in Penn State Football The best players in PSU's football program
Great Players in Notre Dame Football The best players in ND's football program
Great Coaches in Notre Dame Football The best coaches in any football program
Great Players in Alabama Football from Quarterbacks to offensive Linemen Greats!
Great Moments in Alabama Football AU Football from the start. This is the book.
Great Moments in Penn State Football PSU Football, start--games, coaches, players,
Great Moments in Notre Dame Football ND Football, start, games, coaches, players
Cross Country With the Parents A great trip from East Coast to West with the kids
Seniors, Social Security & the Minimum Wage. Things seniors need to know.
How to Write Your First Book and Publish It with CreateSpace
The US Immigration Fix--It's all in here. Finally, an answer.
I had a Dream IBM Could be #1 Again The title is self-explanatory
WineDiets.Com Presents The Wine Diet Learn how to lose weight while having fun.
Wilkes-Barre, PA; Return to Glory Wilkes-Barre City's return to glory
Geoffrey Parsons' Epoch... The Land of Fair Play Better than the original.
The Bill of Rights 4 Dummmies! This is the best book to learn about your rights.
Sol Bloom's Epoch ...Story of the Constitution The best book to learn the Constitution
America 4 Dummmies! All Americans should read to learn about this great country.
The Electoral College 4 Dummmies! How does it really work?
The All-Everything Machine Story about IBM's finest computer server.

Other Brian Kelly books can be found at amazon.com/author/brianwkelly

www.ingramcontent.com/pod-product-compliance
Lightning Source LLC
Chambersburg PA
CBHW061518040426
42450CB00008B/1678